I WAS A STRANGER AND YOU TOOK ME IN

I Was a Stranger and You Took Me In

A Guide for Ministering to Returning Catholics

Loyes M. Spayd

TWENTY-THIRD PUBLICATIONS
twentythirdpublications.com

TWENTY-THIRD PUBLICATIONS
One Montauk Avenue, Suite 200
New London, CT 06320
(860) 437-3012 or (800) 321-0411
www.twentythirdpublications.com

Copyright © 2018 Loyes M. Spayd. All rights reserved. No part of this publication may be reproduced in any manner without prior written permission of the publisher. Write to the Permissions Editor.

Cover photo: © shutterstock.com / releon8211

ISBN: 978-1-62785-345-3
Library of Congress Control Number: 2017958810
Printed in the U.S.A.

DEDICATION

*I dedicate this book
to the memory of
Sr. Anita Sherwood, OSB,
who mentored me
and taught me so much
about how to share
the love of God.*

Contents

Acknowledgments	ix
Introduction	1
Chapter One Why People Leave	3
Chapter Two Why People Long to Return	17
Chapter Three How to Welcome Them Home	31
Chapter Four Pastoral Practices	43
Chapter Five Sharing Our Pastoral Practices with You	63
Chapter Six A Look at Your Pastoral Practices	67
Appendix	80
Resources for Welcoming Home Returning Catholics	82
Bibliography	84

ACKNOWLEDGMENTS

I wish to thank Twenty-Third Publications for giving me the opportunity to write this book.

I wish to thank the people who agreed to let me interview them. Their goal, as is mine, is to help people in their return to the church.

I wish to thank my wonderful friends who encouraged me, supported me, and loved me through this process.

A special thank you to the Benedictine Sisters of Bristow, Virginia, who lavished me with love, prayer, and hospitality as I spent four days writing in their guest house.

And I am grateful for the gift of the returning Catholics who came into my life and taught me courage and showed me the grace of God working in their lives!

INTRODUCTION

I have ministered in the Catholic Church for forty years—as a volunteer, as a professional, and again as a volunteer. One of the many ministries I worked in was service to inactive Catholics who were thinking about returning to an active practice of their faith. In this ministry, especially, I came to see that one needs to tread gently because we are working with people who have broken hearts and wounds. I would venture to say that this is more a ministry of healing than of catechesis. Although catechesis is certainly part of it, we must first invite God to mend and heal.

I have seen this ministry done very well, and I have seen it done poorly. I write this book as an invitation to you who are in parish ministry to do it well. I certainly do not have all the answers, but over the years I have seen and been a part of what works for folks. God bless you as you welcome home the stranger.

Chapter One

WHY PEOPLE LEAVE

"My mother lay dying in the hospital," the woman told me. "She was a devout Catholic all her life, and I know it was important to her to have a priest anoint her and give her viaticum in her final hours. It was the middle of the night, and I called our local Catholic parish and asked them to send a priest as soon as possible. A priest never came! My mother died without the benefit of the sacraments. I was very upset and angry! I haven't been inside a Catholic church since my mom's funeral."

I have heard stories like this many times. There are many possible reasons why a priest didn't come: he didn't receive the message; he fell back to sleep; his car wouldn't start; he got stuck in traffic…who knows? But the perception of this daughter is that the church (generalized from a single member of the clergy) was not there for her when she needed it. Some would say that maybe she was ready to leave the church anyway. Maybe so, but even if that's true, the reasons for that are equally worthy of exploration. We needed to hear and respond to her where she was, and that didn't happen.

Once, when I was a patient in a hospital, a Catholic priest came into my room. He did not introduce himself, nor did he ask me my name. He anointed me (sacrament of the sick) and gave me Eucharist and left without much to say! The whole encounter lasted less than five minutes.

The sacraments are wonderful opportunities for extending the love and warmth of Christ and his church. In the opening example I shared, the dying mother and her daughter may very well have been open to healing and compassion.

In my case, sickness exposed my vulnerability. Ministers have to respect the sick person's dignity and the freedom to say yes or no to what the church offers.

People Whose Parents Drifted

Sometimes people have been born into the faith and received one or more of the sacraments, but are pulled out of active practice by disillusioned or disengaged parents.

Just a few months ago, a woman in our parish RCIA (Rite of Christian Initiation of Adults) process, whom I will call Ann, was confirmed and received first Eucharist. She was born in Vietnam to American parents at the end of the war when all the refugees were leaving. Her father did not want to start the perilous evacuation journey home with his family until she was baptized, so he found a Catholic priest to baptize her when she was six days old. By the time the baptism occurred, they were the second-to-last American family to leave for the States. Not too long after their arrival, the father, never happy about the changes from the Second Vatican Council, became increasingly angry about them. He left the church and took his family with him. Ann's older brother and sister had received their sacraments of initiation, but Ann had only been baptized. When their mother died, Ann and her sister decided to return to the church. Ann came to our RCIA process and completed her sacramental initiation. Her sister was her sponsor. Her brother, although he had not returned to an active practice of the faith, attended his sister's initiation and celebrated with them. I see the women regularly at Mass, and perhaps the brother will someday return. Their father's anger at the church forced them to leave the church, but the death of their mother showed them that they needed faith in their lives.

In the first parish where I worked, I started an RCIA process—a somewhat daring step, since only the 1979 provisional rite had been promulgated. A man came to my office and said he wanted to have his eight-year-old son baptized. The little boy had spent time with Catholic friends, and he wanted what they had. The father had left the Catholic Church many years before. No particular reason was offered; he had just drifted away.

He shared with me that when he was in the army and stationed in Korea, he met and married his wife who was a non-practicing Buddhist. I told him that in order for us to baptize his son he himself would have to return to an active practice of his faith. I didn't know if he was ready to do that. He said he thought he might be. I referred him to the pastor for counseling and spiritual direction and enrolled his son in the RCIA process for children. (This event occurred early in my career and the parish did not have in place a process for returning Catholics, other than to meet with a priest.) His son was fully initiated into the church the following spring, and Dad returned to the church as well. The following year, Mom started the RCIA process, and a year later she was fully initiated into the church. The following year, Dad, only in his early fifties, dropped dead of a heart attack. As sad as the loss of their father and husband was, the little boy and his mom were now part of a faith community that would continue to pray for them and love and support them. And, of course, Dad was now with Jesus! This dad, spurred by his son's search for God and church in his life, had decided he needed to reflect on his own faith journey and return.

People Who Felt Unimportant and Neglected
It is important to make time to help people even when it is inconvenient for us. Sometimes the most significant ministry happens at inconvenient times—they may be invitations from Christ to be present to his people.

I once heard a priest tell this story: "It was late Friday afternoon and I was ready to leave my office and relax a bit before the hectic schedule of the weekend. I was headed to the door when my phone rang. I debated whether or not to answer it. I decided, reluctantly, to answer. There was a young man on the phone, and he said, urgently, 'Father I need to talk to you right away!' I replied, 'What is this about?' The young man answered, curtly, 'Does it matter?' Shamed, I answered, 'No, of course not! Come over right away.'" The priest ended his story by saying, "I never asked that question again."

Sometimes the biggest issues for pastoral ministers are time and energy. I once heard a priest say that our real ministry exists in the interruptions. But if it is Friday or the end of a stressful day, it's often difficult to respond as Christ would. Sadly, sometimes, we do this at the expense of alienating people in need.

People Who Have Felt Condemned or Excluded

The needs and issues of everyone are important, not just those of the people with whom we feel comfortable. Again, at issue is the dignity of the human person.

I was at a workshop for pastoral ministers working in the RCIA process. During one afternoon session, we discussed how to minister effectively to folks with serious issues, such as addictions, divorce and remarriage, or gender identity. At one point in the discussion, one of the attendees spoke up and said, "Let's not just discuss the issues of inquirers, catechumens, and candidates. What about us? Let's be honest—don't we have some of the same issues?" The speaker was a priest who was a recovering alcoholic. Several people began to share their stories and spiritual struggles. Then a young man spoke up and said he was gay. He left the seminary because he did not want to use the priesthood as a "cover" for his sexual orientation. But he asked the poignant question, "Is there room for me in this church?" I wonder how many LGBTQI Catholics feel "at home" in the church.

Human sexuality is a "loaded" emotional, moral, spiritual issue as well as a physical one. Shame and guilt are two feelings the pastoral minister does not want to elicit. Rather, we should welcome people with warmth and hospitality. We need to listen to their stories and experiences; then, in time, we can gently and clearly explain the teachings of the church on human sexuality, not forgetting their nuances.

While it is not possible for us to change the teachings of the church, it is possible for us to invite people to join us in worship at Mass, devotions, and prayer services. If they are in a situation that prevents their reception of the sacraments, they are still welcome to be a part of our community. Invite them to parish activities. If one does not already exist, start a support/prayer group. The goal is for them to experience healing and the love of Jesus Christ from us and the faith community.

Those Who Reject Key Teaching

Sometimes we encounter people who disagree with important teachings of the church, find them irrelevant, or are not willing to make the changes in their lives as a response to these teachings.

In addition to the issue of gender orientation and practice, there is the whole area of the church's teachings on human sexuality. I have taught adolescents and young adults who were amazed and shocked that the church teaches that they could not be sexually active and intimate until they were married. "You've got to be kidding! That's so unrealistic! That's just plain medieval!" were some of the responses I received. They (and some adults) see the church as rigid and out of touch with today's culture.

Some people have left because of the pedophilia scandal and/or have been victims of sexual abuse. It is difficult for some to believe there is sin in the church. Sin has existed in the church since its beginnings because there are flawed human beings in the church. Thank God (literally) that the Holy Spirit has ensured the church's survival.

I have worked in the RCIA process for four decades. I have

met and ministered to numerous individuals and couples who were divorced and remarried and struggled with the annulment process. Some went through the process of waiting and received their annulments. They entered the church even though their conversion and readiness to become Catholic happened long before the annulment was final. Some folks became discouraged and left the RCIA process. Some Catholics I know left an active practice of the faith because they felt the church's teaching on divorce and remarriage was punitive and the annulment process was too painful, unwieldy, and complicated.

Once again, we cannot change the teachings of the church on marriage, but we can welcome and love. In my experience, many Catholics do not know the teachings, or if they do, they do not understand them or are misinformed about them. For example, it is important to clarify the status of the marriage.

I met with a mother who wanted her daughter, age ten, to receive the sacraments of reconciliation and Eucharist for the first time. When I inquired about her own faith life, she burst into tears and sobbed. She said she hadn't received Communion in several years. When I gently asked her why, she responded, "Because I am divorced!" I asked her if she had remarried, and she said she had not. I had the delightful task of telling her that she was welcome to receive reconciliation and Eucharist herself because she had not remarried. Divorce is not a mortal sin. She replied that she had been taught that divorce excommunicated her from the church. "No," I said. "You were misinformed. Welcome back!"

In some cases, such as a lack of form, a simple paperwork process and a validation ceremony is all that may be needed.

If in fact the couple does need an annulment, then inform

them about the process. Put them in the care of someone who will guide them—someone such as an advocate priest or deacon, or a lay person who has been trained in canon law. Invite them to participate in parish activities—especially a support group for the divorced. Give them pamphlets to read.

Invite someone trained in the process and canon law to come to the parish to give a talk, followed by a question and answer period and perhaps some faith sharing. These couples may have children who have not, or not often, participated in a faith community. Help them to enroll their children in faith formation or an RCIA process adapted for children. Invite the children to participate in children's liturgy of the word (if they are not in RCIA). There should be no guilt or censure imposed on these parents—just help, support, and education. I have been privileged to be a part of and witnessed so much healing and joy. Often miracles happen in the lives of these couples and families.

The Frustrated Faithful Dissenters

I once interviewed for a diocesan job in religious education. The cardinal who was interviewing me said that if Catholics knew the beliefs and teachings of the church, they would not leave. I am convinced this statement is not entirely true. I know some well-informed Catholics who have left.

Those Who Have Wandered Off

Some folks just drift away from an active practice of the faith. Often people do not see the teachings and practices of the church as relevant to their lives, to the issues with which they struggle. Some say they don't have time. Many have not experienced a close intimate relationship with Jesus Christ and the faith community.

One friend said to me, "I was happy being 'bad'; I didn't need the church." Many years later she started attending Mass. She would not talk to anyone, because she felt guilty and felt like she really didn't belong. Then one day she decided she would volunteer to clean the church. She figured she was at least worthy enough to do menial tasks. Eventually she worked up the courage to attend some of the social events of the 50+ Club (a social club for seniors). She made some friends and realized that no one was judging her, and she began to feel like she belonged to the community. She felt herself growing closer to God, and she returned to the sacraments. The pastor, with whom she had a few conversations, invited her to sit on the pastoral council. She was overwhelmed but accepted.

Eventually, the coordinator of the RCIA process invited her to be a sponsor. After a lot of encouragement from members of the team, she agreed. Being a sponsor was, in her words, a life-changing experience. She learned and grew in her faith. She then had a severe emotional crisis that involved her having flashbacks of physical and emotional abuse in her childhood. These were memories she had repressed for many years. She went to see the pastor. He met with her frequently and strongly suggested she see a therapist. He recommended one from the parish. She began therapy and shared her situation with a couple of us on the RCIA team. We were very supportive and prayed with her and for her.

She is a wonderful sponsor and now attends daily Mass and continues with parish ministry. She is still in therapy but is gradually healing and has found much peace and joy in her life. Her goal now is to raise the awareness of church leadership about the frequency and severity of abuse of children. When she was a child being abused, she attended Catholic school and now realizes that the faculty (professed religious) was aware that something was wrong in her life but did nothing about it. Of course, many years ago, church educators were not educated themselves on how to handle and report abuse. My friend is a "walking miracle" now. I went to Central Europe with our parish choir and invited her to come and to be my roommate on the trip. She had a wonderful time and made many new friends. It has been such a blessing to see this woman blossom in her relationship with Jesus Christ and the church. She is now a member of the RCIA team and a Sunday dismissal catechist.

Those Restrained by Fear or Shame

Recently, I was serving on a retreat team, and one woman, raised Catholic and a junior in college, said to me, "I didn't feel good enough and worthy to go to church!" This young woman had a difficult family life, a tremendous amount of responsibility, and was trying to live up to her family's cultural expectations of "what a good daughter should be." She also suffered from serious, chronic depression. Many of us on the retreat team spent a lot of time talking to her and praying with her. At the end of the retreat (four days) she felt much better about herself and agreed to see a therapist and her campus minister.

Another woman, now in her early thirties, had an out-of-wedlock child at the age of seventeen. Her parents, whom I know, were very active in the church. She said, "I felt such shame and guilt that I couldn't go to church. I felt I was an embarrassment to myself and my parents." Her parents, extended family, and friends supported her and encouraged her to return to the church and the sacraments. After several months, she started to attend Mass and eventually returned to reception of the sacraments. She said the most healing experience she had was that nobody, especially the parish priests and parishioners, judged her. They all simply loved her and supported her in her new role as a single mother. She eventually married the father of her child, had another child, and she and her family are active in the church. She wants to help other young adults return to the church.

In one parish where I worked, I started an RCIA process for children of catechetical age. Some of these children had parents entering the church, but most had parents who had left the church. These parents delayed presenting their children for the sacraments because the parents felt shame and guilt and were afraid of being judged and rejected. And, in some parishes, they were. The pastor of this parish gave me permission to start the RCIA process for children but said to me, "I don't want to deal with those parents who are angry at the church." I replied, "But they come to us because the word on the street is that here they will be welcomed and treated with respect, dignity, and mercy." Later, this dear man would brag about all the families returning to the church.

Those Made to Feel Different
A basic belief of our faith is respect and care for the dignity of every human person. This belief obviously includes those who have a physical and/or an intellectual disability. Many parents of children with disabilities stay away from the church because

they think the church has nothing to offer them. Education, marketing, and publicity are very much needed in this area of ministry. Many (most) parishes have now made their physical buildings accessible, but we need to make our worship, sacraments, and catechesis accessible as well. An intellectual disability should never be an obstacle to receiving the sacraments. God can and does reveal himself to children and adults with disabilities. We sometimes have a tendency "to limit God."

Because some of these children are nonverbal and/or do not have a fully developed sense of right and wrong, their parents assume their children cannot receive penance, Eucharist, and confirmation. Many years ago, Cardinal Joseph Bernardin, archbishop of Chicago, wrote a pastoral letter encouraging access to the sacraments for all persons with intellectual disabilities. I remember the day I told a mother that her nonverbal, twelve-year-old daughter was welcome to receive the Eucharist. Once again, I was embracing a weeping mother. There is no disability that God cannot break through.

Again, there is a need to educate our people and, in some cases, change our own attitudes about inclusivity in our church for people with disabilities. Early in my ministry, a woman whose son had a severe learning disability came into my office. She was very angry and lambasted me for not providing a good supportive learning environment for her son. She had been given the "run around" by the public school system, and she expected the same treatment from me. She had left the church, but she wanted her son to have a learning experience that respected him and would help him with his disability.

I gave her time to calm down, and then we discussed options for her son. The intermediate step was to place her son in the RCIA for children. Her son was already baptized, so this placement was a stopgap measure, not an appropriate permanent solution. We discussed the need for a religious education program for children like her son. There was a diocesan program but no program for children with special learning needs in our region, so I started one in our parish. The diocese supported us and provided the training for me and the catechists. Her son was enrolled in SPRED (Special Religious Education Development), and she became the volunteer director. She also returned to the church. To this day, that program is still running and, almost thirty years later, she and I are the best of friends. Patient listening and a warm welcome helped to create the environment for a solution.

There are catechetical and liturgical programs written specifically for people with disabilities. Rose Kennedy, who had a child with an intellectual disability, wrote a catechetical program. Jean Vanier, who is well-known for his L'Arche communities, brought the catechetical process SPRED, mentioned earlier, to the United States and originally based it in the Archdiocese of Chicago. It is now available to any diocese—the program and the appropriate training. I started this program in two parishes. Some dioceses have offices or departments for special religious education and offices for persons with disabilities. Their trained staff can be very helpful to local parishes. The gospels have numerous stories in which Jesus reaches out and heals persons with disabilities. As in all situations, he sets a model for us to follow.

As you read these stories, a few of your own may come to mind. It is rare that people leave for no reason. As I have mentioned earlier, people leave because they do not feel they have been treated with respect, or they sense a lack of compassion on our part. Parents drift away and do not raise their children in the faith. As ministers, we are not always willing to share our time or our own vulnerability. We sometimes show lack of sensitivity when dealing with issues of sexuality, marriage and divorce, and abuse of all kinds. And sometimes we are restrained by our own fear and shame. As ministers, we are not perfect but we do need to do some reflection, even perhaps with a spiritual director, about what we can do to open our minds and hearts and minister more effectively.

In the next chapter, I will discuss some of the reasons why people who have left an active practice of their faith now long to return.

Chapter Two

WHY PEOPLE LONG TO RETURN

There is, as Fr. Ronald Rolheiser wrote in his book *The Holy Longing*, a longing that exists within each of us. St. Augustine in his *Confessions* wrote, "Our hearts are restless until they rest in you."

Whether we are conscious of it or not, we spend our entire lives trying to fill that longing—that empty space within us. Some people unsuccessfully try to fill that empty space with drugs, alcohol, food, sex, money, possessions, and power—often ending up addicted. Even in healthy relationships there can still be within us the feeling that something is missing. No one human person can totally fulfill that longing. St. Francis de Sales said that we do not experience true peace, joy, and fulfillment until our hearts are one with the heart of Christ.

Some significant life events can cause us to ask: Is this all there is? What happened to my goals and dreams? I didn't get the job or promotion I wanted. My marriage was supposed to last forever. My children are not perfect. My child or spouse or friend was not supposed to die of cancer. Like Job we will say to God, "But I am a good person, why me?" I once asked that question to a spiritual director, and his answer to me was, "Why not you?" Not exactly the answer I wanted to hear, but I got the message. My spiritual director was trying to tell me that none of us escapes the trials of life.

Two great books that deal with this topic are John Aurelio's *Mosquitoes in Paradise* and Rabbi Kushner's *Why Do Bad Things Happen to Good People?* Aurelio was serving as a priest on the staff of a home for children with severe birth defects and intellectual disabilities. Parents and staff members confronted him with questions about why these innocent children should suffer like this—Is God that cruel? God does not create this suffering, but he does, in the midst of it, show his great love in so many ways.

Rabbi Kushner wrote his book after his son developed a very serious illness. Kushner confronted what he described in himself, before his son's illness, as self-righteous and judgmental attitudes toward his congregation members dealing with misfortune. His son taught him to love people unconditionally and be with them in their pain.

I worked as a director of religious education in a parish in Northern Virginia, just outside Washington, DC. Most of the population there has it all—wealth, power, influence, fame. In both the RCIA and the Welcome Home Process, many of the people who came were admirals, generals, diplomats, and

World Bank employees. A surprising number of them said, "I have it all, but I am unhappy—something in my life is missing. Can you help me?"

Betsy, twenty-four years old, was away from the church for eleven years. Her mother did not practice any religion, and her father had converted to Catholicism. Her paternal grandparents were, as she described them "mean" but practicing Catholics.

Even as a young child she noticed the difference between her father's and grandparents' behavior and the Catholic beliefs they professed. She was turned off by what she saw as hypocrisy. Her parents separated when she was twelve years old. Her father was addicted to drugs and unfaithful to her mother. He was a medical doctor and considered himself a pillar of the community, but he eventually lost his medical license. Betsy saw hypocrisy and meanness of spirit in "good Catholics." She left the church.

As Betsy grew older, she realized that the church might have more to offer her than what she had experienced as a child. She said that her religious education as a youngster was "fluff" but also realized that the church was bigger than her experience of religious education and the behavior of her family. She felt she needed a faith that would fill her adult longings. She felt the need for faith and a faith community.

She started to attend young adult sessions at a parish near to ours. She found out about the Landings Program, a program for returning Catholics sponsored by the Paulist Fathers. She completed the program and returned to the church. In the program, she met her husband, whom she describes as a very devout Catholic. She said she benefited greatly from the small-group sharing in the Landings Program. Hearing other people's personal stories and sharing her own helped her to change her opinions. Also, she was older and ready to make a more mature decision. When she and her husband decided to start a family, she experienced some fertility issues. She eventually became pregnant with a little boy. The pregnancy was a healthy one, but there were serious complications with the labor and delivery of her son. As a result, the baby suffered brain trauma and lived only sixteen hours. She was devastated, but she said, "I could not have survived this ordeal if it were not for my faith, my husband's faith, and the support of our church community." She now has a healthy two-year-old girl. She readily agreed to my request for an interview because she wanted to share her story so that others could be helped in their journey.

I also think of Sue, a woman in her mid-sixties and retired. She grew up in a traditional Catholic parish. She left the church when she was in college. She didn't see the Catholic faith having much of an impact on her life. She became a nurse and worked weekends, so she didn't attend Mass. She married a man who was not practicing his Catholic faith. Every once in a while, she said, they went to Mass. She had her first three children baptized Catholic but, "by the time the fourth child arrived, I was overwhelmed and there was no baptism." Her husband started searching for a church where he felt at home. The family attended a Unity church for a while. The turning point for her was 9/11. She started "shopping" for Catholic churches.

After forty-three years of marriage, her husband had an affair and left her. They divorced. She became very sick and consumed with guilt.

She came to my parish and attended the Welcome Home Program. She was not comfortable with the personal sharing, so she attended only one session. She was, however, invited to attend the Little Rock Scripture Program, and she loves it.

Sue now has been participating in the Bible study program with us for fifteen years, even though she now worships at a different parish. She is a very bright, intellectual woman; she studies the writings of Jung and Buddhism and struggles with the issues and relationship of science and faith. But, she says, "I can relate to the teachings of the church on sacrifice. We are on a path, and at our core it's about peace. I will never give up the Catholic Church."

I think Sue was one of those persons who as a young adult did not find the Catholic faith relevant to her young life. She then married, pursued her career, and raised her children. The cruelty, violence, and senselessness of 9/11 impelled her to look inward to her spiritual life, and her first step was to reach out to a church—the Catholic Church from her childhood. Also, the failure of her marriage was a devastating blow. The combined events made her aware that she needed a relationship with God and a sustaining faith in her life.

Both Sue and Betsy have experienced pain and sorrow and its impact on their lives, but the Welcome Home approach was different for each woman, and we, as ministers, need to be tuned into that. Our young woman was ready for the intimacy of a small faith community, whereas our older woman was more comfortable with an intellectual approach. Neither woman is wrong—each found the approach that worked for her. They both found a relationship with Jesus Christ and his church, and peace in their lives, and that is all that matters.

Lucy was in her forties. She was baptized Catholic and received her first Communion. Her mother was divorced and did not feel welcome in the Catholic Church because of her divorce. After her first Communion, Lucy had no experience of church, but she did think that she still had God in her life. She says that she did not lead a very moral life. She moved to Virginia to make a fresh start but still felt that something was missing. She went to work in a restaurant and met a young woman on staff there who was a devout Catholic. Lucy said to this young woman, "I want what you have!" Her friend invited Lucy to a Bible study, and later she attended a Life in the Spirit seminar and gave her life to God. She joined the charismatic prayer group.

Lucy made an appointment to go to confession. Before she went, she made a long list of all her sins and read the gospel story of the prodigal son. The sacrament was a wonderful experience for her. The priest suggested that they read and discuss the story of the prodigal son. Lucy was amazed that the priest picked the same Scripture she had read earlier. She and the priest talked and prayed. She felt like she was with a good friend. The priest told her to go to communion and follow her heart.

At age thirty-five, Lucy received the sacrament of confirmation. Her first marriage was annulled, and she married her second husband in the church. She continues to be part of the prayer group and serves in several ministries. Lucy says she now wants to return the love she received and help the church. She works with adolescents. She has worked at the same restaurant for twenty-three years, and the owners allow her to use the restaurant for evangelization. Every Monday night, the restaurant, under Lucy's management, offers "Faith and Food." They serve food, bring in a speaker and have faith discussions. A lot of young people attend. Lucy says, "Christ is in the house."

Note the elements in Lucy's return and conversion. She witnessed the faith of a coworker, who invited her to church for a Bible study. She found knowledge and a faith community. She then moved on to a Life in the Spirit seminar, where she deepened her relationship with Christ and a faith community. She then was ready to participate in the sacramental life of the church. And her experience of penance was like the prodigal son (daughter) as she experienced God's love and mercy through the ministry of a sensitive and skilled priest. Lucy, now having experienced God's love and forgiveness, was ready to move on and live her baptismal mission by evangelizing youth.

Lucy had experienced her mother's rejection by the church. She received no faith formation as a child, and that left a vacuum in her life; as she grew older she felt that something was missing. She had no moral code to guide her.

She recognized that her friend's invitation was a pathway to God and something that she needed. Her experience of a faith community, especially their love, made her aware of this need in her life. Her positive and loving experience of the church's sacrament of penance sealed the deal for her. Lucy, like the Samaritan woman, now forgiven, healed, and loved, could go forth to begin the work of evangelizing others.

A Latino couple came to the parish and wanted to have their two daughters, ages seven and ten, baptized. The couple were fully initiated Catholics but hadn't practiced their faith in many years. Although their children spoke English, mom and dad, having come from El Salvador, wanted a Spanish program. In this particular parish, the RCIA process for children was bilingual. This process was intergenerational catechesis and used sponsor families. Their children were fully initiated, and the faith of their parents blossomed. They not only returned to the church but became very active in ministry. They became RCIA sponsors and served on the pastoral council. Mom went to work for the church in the parish office, and dad studied to become a deacon and was later ordained. The little girl, who was ten at her baptism, is now twenty-four and is sponsoring another Latino young adult in the RCIA. Sensitivity to language and culture was key in this family's journey.

This couple's initial motivation to come to the church was to seek sacraments for their children. Reception of the sacraments is an important tradition in their culture. What this couple, Carlo and Anna, did not expect was that the process for their children also involved them, and they realized that they too needed a relationship with Jesus and his church. They were touched by the Holy Spirit and responded to this love by dedicating their lives to service in the church.

Shortly before I retired, an older woman, Nancy, came in to the parish office to talk to me. She was thinking of returning to the church. This woman had traveled frequently, and she was planning another trip overseas, but this time she was fearful. She felt she needed to go to confession before she made the trip. She was afraid that if something happened to her and she died, she would be damned because she had left the church and had not been to confession for several years.

I was unable to spend a lot of time with her on that first visit because I had a family commitment. I made an appointment for her to return. I wondered if she would keep the appointment, but she did. And she told me her story. She had been married for forty years, and her husband was emotionally and physically abusive. She had stayed in the marriage because she had been taught that she could not be a Catholic if she was divorced. On one occasion, she decided to visit a nearby monastery and consult with a priest. The priest told her to "pull herself up by her bootstraps and go back to the marriage." She was very angry and hurt.

She left the church and divorced her husband. A few years later she remarried. I counseled her and referred her to our pastor. The next day she called the parish to make an appointment with the pastor, and he himself answered the phone. Anyone who has worked for a parish knows that the pastor rarely answers the parish phone line. She explained her situation and he told her to come in, that he would see her right away.

I retired shortly after that and I did not hear from her for a while. Then I got a phone call from her, and she said that she had returned to the sacraments and was very happy and peaceful. I do not know what the pastor said to her or what happened after that, and I did not ask. I was just very happy for her. I do know that my seeing her a second time and the pastor's answering the phone and inviting her to come immediately were definite signs to her that we (and God) cared for her and wished to help her. Nancy moved from the guilt and fear of punishment to a joyful reception of the sacraments and a life of peace and joy.

My last story here is about a woman I met at the parish I am in now. I had heard that she had left the church and come back. I approached her, told her about the book I was writing, and asked her if she would tell me her story for my book. I promised I would not use her real name. She (I am going to call her Angela) said she would be happy to help, especially if her story helped someone thinking of returning to the church or those ministering to those who were.

Angela grew up in a "very Catholic family." She attended a Catholic grade school run by the Daughters of Charity. Her father was an alcoholic but quit drinking when she was born, and, she noted, her family didn't talk about "things like that."

When it was time for her to go to college she was only interested in booze and boys. She decided to attend college in the town where her uncle owned a beer distributorship. Her uncle was also Catholic and very active in his parish. He showed her around all the local pubs and told the owners to "take care of his niece," which meant giving her two free pitchers of beer whenever she walked in. The college was also near a military air base, which, of course, meant there were plenty of boys. Angela was all set. In her college years, she played hard and became an alcoholic. She made feeble attempts to go back to church, but her attempts were not successful. When her father died, she felt a great hole, but still she did not go to church.

Work brought her to the Northern Virginia area. She went to one Catholic church in the area but it was an interfaith center. She did not feel comfortable there because it did not feel like a sacred space. A year later, she tried another parish but the priest there was too dogmatic for her.

She became engaged and went to see a priest about being married in the church. The priest had spent some time with her and her fiancé, and he did not want to marry them because he did not think the marriage would be successful. Also, her fiancé had been married before. The priest advised her to marry in a Protestant church because that would make it easier for her to get an annulment if the marriage failed, which he was convinced it would.

In this marriage, Angela was emotionally and physically abused by her husband. Four years later, she filed for divorce, and this same priest helped her to get an annulment. She still, however, did not return to the church.

Seventeen years later, she came back to the church. By then she was sober and attending AA meetings regularly. Angela was a golfer and an avid fan of Payne Stewart, who was a professional golfer touring with the Professional Golfers Association (PGA). He and two other golfers were killed in a plane crash in 1999. Payne's two companions on the plane were Christians and members of a Bible study in the PGA. They had invited Payne to join them in the Bible study. Not long before the crash, Payne had committed his life to Jesus Christ and joined the Baptist church. He apparently changed from being a vicious and sarcastic competitor to a man who was peaceful and joyful.

Angela was so moved by the testimony given at Payne's funeral that she made the decision to return to the church. She walked into the nave of our church and sat there for three hours and sobbed. She finally asked a staff member where the priests' offices were—she was going to go in and just make an appointment to see a priest. A young man in jeans and a plaid shirt came out and asked if he could help her. She told him that she wanted to make an appointment to talk with a priest. The young man said, "I am a priest; you can talk to me." Angela had never seen a priest not wearing clerical garb, and he looked so young. Angela started to sob and the priest said, "Let's go have a cup of coffee and talk."

Angela said she had a huge hole in her heart, and she had tried everything else to make it go away. The priest spent over an hour with her, gave her a Bible to take home, and suggested she stop at the local Catholic bookstore and buy some music she would enjoy (Angela was a singer). She met with this young priest once a week for a year. At his suggestion, she went to the 7:30 AM Mass the following Sunday. She sat in the back. After Mass and much deliberation, she decided to go to the parish hall for some coffee and donuts. She didn't want anybody to touch her or talk to her, but then she found herself talking to a couple who looked friendly, and she told them this was her first time back to the church in many years. This couple warmly welcomed her, got her some coffee, and invited her to sit at a table with them. Angela then blurted out her story. Angela felt so relieved and loved, and she realized that nobody was going to hate her. She and that couple became great friends.

Angela returned to the sacraments and became very active in the parish. She attended a Bible study, coordinated the Little Rock Scripture Study, became an RCIA sponsor, and ran the inquiry phase of RCIA. She served on the pastoral council twice. Today she is a part-time parish employee and compiles the bulletin every week. Angela has been sober for thirty-four years and active in the church for eighteen years. She is happy and joyful living out what she now knows is God's mission for her.

As a child, Angela was formed in the Catholic faith but rejected it. The addiction to alcohol and an abusive marriage left her a very wounded and lonely person. But God, who is a persistent "Hound of Heaven," kept exposing Angela to kind and loving people of God so that, at long last, she fully opened her heart and walked through the doors of the church into the arms of loving Catholics (and a loving Christ), and she has never left.

No one can prevent life's stresses and dire events from happening, but what we the church can offer is a path to find a relationship with Jesus Christ and his faith community.

We cannot always prevent tragedies and unhappiness from happening to us but Christ and his church walk with us at these times. We can assure people that Christ will walk with them through all the circumstances of their lives. We can offer them a community that will cry with them and celebrate with them. We and Christ can offer them the peace for which they long.

The journey is not always easy—sometimes it is difficult for them to trust, to be vulnerable, and to accept the gift of faith. We can also assure them that God has called them to seek a return. God has planted that desire in their hearts. God loved them first, and he is simply waiting for them to love him back.

Chapter Three

How to Welcome Them Home

Here is a sample bulletin announcement:

> We at our parish welcome your return. Whatever your situation, we welcome you and will listen attentively and respectfully to your concerns and feelings with acceptance and without judgment. There will be no pressure or anticipated commitments of any type. There is a group of Catholics here who have struggled with faith, and in some cases have been away from the church for an extended period of time.
>
> For some, after time away, their understanding of the Catholic faith may be incomplete or may include misinformation. Or perhaps you may have specific questions

regarding church teachings. We want to provide a forum where issues of faith and doubt can be honestly and openly addressed. We can also provide excellent catechetical resources if you would like them.

Please contact: [information on contact staff person or coordinator].

BULLETIN FROM ST. JOHN NEUMANN CATHOLIC CHURCH, RESTON, VA

The reader may wonder what good a bulletin announcement like this can do. The people who may want to read it are not going to Mass. That may or may not be true, but the burden for issuing the invitation and disseminating the information belongs to all of us—staff and active churchgoers.

I offer this bulletin announcement because it is warm and welcoming. It sets the tone for what the process will be like. The welcoming process needs to be healing and uplifting. The person returning, or contemplating a return, needs the time, safety, and trust to share his/her story. And the minister's job is to have a prayerful, listening heart. In time, the person may be ready to return to the sacramental life of the church, but that is one of the last steps for them to take.

In this chapter, I describe the baptismal catechumenate process as a means of catechesis and formation for those thinking of a return to the church. This process invites them to tell their story—why they left, where they have been, why they are thinking of returning, and their hopes and dreams for the future. It is an adult learning process (not lecture) that respects their adult faith journey. The process references their baptism because it is at their baptism that they first committed to their faith (or someone promised to raise them in the faith) and now they need to recommit to that baptismal way of life.

The catechumenal method is meant to be the model for all catechesis. This is not my idea, but a statement in the *General Directory for Catechesis* (GDC, 90). The catechumenal process is humanizing, compassionate, realistic, and respectful of the adult learning process and the adult faith journey. It can be used effectively in facilitating one's return to the church.

(This is *not* to say that people seeking a return to the church should be included in the RCIA process; the Rite of Christian Initiation of Adults is a process for people seeking entrance into the Catholic faith, or seeking to complete their initiation. The two groups are coming from different places and often have different issues that need to be addressed. I am also not recommending a "slavish imitation" [GDC, 91] of the model, for that would be an injustice to the RCIA process itself and not helpful to returning Catholics. But the principles of the process have proven to be invaluable to the adult learning and spiritual formation process.)

The RCIA in its provisional form was released by the Vatican in 1979. Its use for the initiation of adults (and Part Two for children) was mandated in the United States by our bishops in 1988.

The *General Directory for Catechesis* was published by the Vatican in 1997. By the time this significant catechetical document was released for use in the universal church, the accumulated wisdom of the writers was evident:

> Given that the *missio ad gentes* is the paradigm of all the Church's missionary activity, the baptismal catechumenate, which is joined to it, is the model of its catechizing activity. **GDC, 90**

The GDC goes on to distinguish between pre-baptismal and post-baptismal catechesis.

> The latter derives from the sacraments of initiation which were received as infants [or later], "who have already been introduced into the Church and have been made sons [and daughters] of God by means of Baptism. The basis of their conversion is the Baptism which they have already received and whose power they must develop" [RCIA, 295].
>
> In view of this substantial difference, some elements of the baptismal catechumenate are now considered as the source of inspiration for post-baptismal catechesis.
>
> GDC, 90–91

For those of us who have been doing pre- and post-baptismal catechesis for many years, this statement in a Roman document was a welcome affirmation not only of our opinions but our praxis.

Ten years before the publication of the GDC, Fr. Patrick Brennan, in his well-known book *The Evangelizing Parish*, described lessons the parish can learn from the catechumenate.

- *Conversion takes time*—tell them that conversion takes time.
- *The parish should focus on adults.*
- *Sacraments are about conversion*—they celebrate their conversion.
- *Small is beautiful.*
- *Ministers and ministries can function cooperatively.*

- *The community is the sacrament of God's presence*, and you will experience this.
- *Spirituality is paschal in nature*—the paschal mystery is the celebration of the death and resurrection of Jesus Christ, which we celebrate not only at Mass but also in their lives—their daily dyings (bad times) and risings (good times); Christ and his church will be with them for both.
- *Conversion is the work of the Holy Spirit*—and the Spirit will help you to discern where God is in your life and what he is calling you to be.
- *There is a mutuality in true ministry (all are called to conversion)*.
- *Discernment is a vital part of conversion.*

  ◉ BRENNAN, PP. 12-13

In various documents the church has presented some foundational principles. Here are some of them, and how we put them into practice.

- Our encounters with God through sacraments, liturgy, and Scripture nurture and transform us. *We will reacquaint ourselves with the Mass, the sacraments, and Christ's word.*
- Catechesis is about relationships with Christ and his church. *We will help you to grow stronger in these relationships. We will let you know and affirm that you belong to us and that our community is richer because of your presence and your gifts.*
- Sunday liturgy is central to our faith. *You will come to see*

that the church's story is also your story.
- Our faith is to be celebrated and reflected within the flow and rhythm of the liturgical year. *As we celebrate the rhythm of this year we will continue to encounter Christ and his life.*
- *A faith learned is a faith lived.*

Here are some important values that go with these foundational principles:

- The community is stronger and holier as the result of the growing faith and commitment.
- In the witnessing of our faith we bring others to Christ.
- Faith brings meaning and purpose to our lives.
- It is important for people to feel that they belong.

Now the question is, how do these principles relate to someone who is baptized Catholic and possibly returning to the Catholic Church? All catechesis is oriented to baptism, so this includes formation for returning Catholics. As staff members, we need to review all the implications of baptism so we can break it open for our returnees. What does baptism mean for us and for them?

Baptism begins our relationship with God the Father, Jesus, the Holy Spirit, and the church. It is a relationship between the beloved and the lover. This last idea may possibly be new for to some of our folks.

I once facilitated a retreat for catechists in the Archdiocese of Baltimore. As the basic theme of the retreat, I used the story of the Samaritan woman at the well from the fourth chapter of John's gospel (John 4:4–42). This is the gospel used for the First Scrutiny. Although Jesus told the woman that he knew of her lifestyle (having five husbands), he did not heap shame or guilt on her. What he did was offer her the Living Water that she could not find in her life. He told her that if she drinks of the Living Water he is offering her, she will never thirst again. For their reflection time, I asked the group to think about Jesus' great love for the woman even though she was a sinner, and to think about Jesus' great love for each of them.

At the break, a woman whom I guessed to be in her forties, came up to me sobbing. She said, "I have had many years of religious education and no one has ever told me Jesus loved me." Now maybe someone *had* told her this—who knows?—but that love was not a reality she had experienced.

Folks returning to the church may not understand and/or have not experienced that invitation to live in God's love. One of the Scriptures I use is 1 John 4:19: "We love because he first loved us," and Psalm 139:13: "You formed me in my inmost being; You knit me in my mother's womb."

Baptism launches us on the journey of responding to and growing in God's love. God has called the inactive folks to a return to his church. He wants them. He wants what is best for them. He wants them to experience lasting peace and joy. The first step in the process is to help them get in touch with that reality. We, the ministers of that love, must stand ready to embrace and support them. Conversion to Christ is not a one-time event; it is an ongoing process as we live out the reality of the paschal mystery in our own lives. They, like us, have had and will continue to have "deaths" and "resurrections" in life. The good news is that they, like Jesus and thanks to Jesus, will rise from these "deaths"—the big ones and the little ones. They will sin and fail and pick themselves back up again. And the second piece of good news is that they do not do this alone.

They are baptized into community, and we are all on the same journey. If they have not been satisfied or successful on this journey alone (probably not), then hopefully they will with us.

The baptismal catechumenate is centered on the liturgy, where we celebrate the paschal mystery that Jesus experienced for us. At the eucharistic liturgy, we unite our paschal mystery with him. As Jesus offered his life to God for us, we too bring our lives, along with the rest of the assembly, and place them on the altar. We offer them to Jesus. All we do is for him. We will struggle with that, but we ask that we, along with the bread and wine, may be transformed, to be ever more like him.

The baptismal catechumenate is grounded in the liturgical year. The celebrations of the liturgical year are for all of us, not just those preparing to enter the church. During the liturgical year we encounter and "break open" the mysteries and tenets of our faith. The liturgy is about God and us. During Advent, we prepare ourselves for the feast of the Incarnation, and during the Christmas season we celebrate it. What does the Incarnation—the fact that Jesus is human and divine—mean to you? He is God, but he felt every emotion you do. He knew grief, sadness, disappointment, anger, frustration, abandonment, fear, temptation, and betrayal. After Christmas, we experience a season of Ordinary Time, and through the six weeks of Lent we prepare for the renewal of our baptismal promises and what they mean for our journey of faith. We have the great celebrations of the Triduum, the Easter season, and a second period of Ordinary Time, ending in the great feast of Christ the King.

We can journey through the liturgical year with our returnees. There are numerous catechetical and transformative moments as they encounter or reacquaint themselves with the patriarchs and prophets of the Hebrew Scriptures; those promises and God's covenant are also for them and all of us. We journey with Jesus through the gospels, with Paul through the beginning of the church, and with the letters of the apostles and the young but growing Christian communities. Through all this, we can help the returnees to answer the big question: "What is the message for me, for my life?"

The baptismal catechumenate is grounded in the life and mission of the community. Before Jesus ascended to the Father, he instructed his apostles to continue the mission he had started. The mission was to proclaim the gospel to all, to build the kingdom of God. We are baptized into that same mission; that mission belongs to the clergy, to the vowed religious, and to *all* of us. Sometimes it is difficult to realize we have the responsibility to live that mission. By serving the other and not just ourselves, we will really find the lasting peace for which we search. However, helping our returning folks to discern where and how God is calling them to serve is a gradual process and not a directive on our part. Part of their formation can be to explore opportunities with them, what appeals to them, what are their gifts. Invite and accompany them to a parish service event.

The baptismal catechumenate is respectful of culture. I live in a very diverse cultural area. This area has a high number of Latinos, Africans, Asians, Indians, and because of the embassies, the World Bank, and the activities of the nation's capital, there are residents from all over the world. Because of this diverse population, my colleagues and I have to be very sensitive to the practices of the various cultures our parishioners and visitors represent. It is not a good idea to impose our specific spiritualities on folks finding their spiritual way. Nor is it good to ignore their culture or impose our American, Western values. Their culture is part of their story—of who they are. When I was in college, I worked one summer as a Maryknoll lay missionary with the Aztec Indians. I discovered that the Aztecs still sang the songs, danced the dances, and used the musical instruments that generations had used to worship the Aztec gods. Today, these songs, dances, and music are used to worship God, Jesus, and the Holy Spirit. The Franciscan missionaries who brought Christianity to Mexico hundreds of years ago encouraged the Indians to do this. When I attended Mass in San Antonio, Texas, a Mariachi band provided the liturgical music. When the Pope John Paul II Cultural Center (now the St. John Paul II National Shrine) first opened in Washington, DC, it had videos of liturgical celebrations from all over the world. I was particularly fascinated by how different countries celebrated the Triduum—strong evidence of the joy and diversity of our universal church.

As parish staffs, we also need to be aware of and sensitive to generational cultures. What speaks to me as a "baby boomer" is not necessarily going to appeal to Generations X, Y, or Z. We will respect each generation and respond to the issues they face. The message of the gospels is timeless, but it does have to be enculturated—it needs to speak to each generation in a way that is relevant to its members.

These principles of the baptismal catechumenate offer an entire curriculum—the traditions, Scriptures, and rituals of our church—for the formation and reformation of our folks seeking to return. The goal for all of us, including our returning Catholics, is conversion leading to transformation. A very wise priest, Fr. James Dunning, one of the founders of the North American Forum on the Catechumenate, would often say that conversion happens when "their story" and the church's story become one—when a person sees himself or herself as an integral part of the great story of salvation.

Chapter Four

Pastoral Practices

Two important practices, among others, for parishes to keep in mind when ministering to returning Catholics are hospitality and forgiveness. Remember the story of Abraham (Genesis 18:1–15) in which he lavishly and generously entertains three guests (whom he did not know) at his home. He treated them as he would treat God, which, it turns out, one of these visitors was.

When we are welcoming people, we need to reach out, be hospitable, and bring them into our world, our culture, with no strings attached. We need to show the same unconditional love Jesus has for us. The Benedictines are known for their charisms of hospitality and forgiveness. Less than an hour from the nation's capital is a Benedictine monastery for women. A few years ago, three of their sisters were hit by a drunk driver as they were returning from a trip to Richmond. One sister died, and the other two were critically injured and endured months of surgeries and rehabilitation. When the driver and his family were identified, the sisters immediately reached out to them to offer forgiveness. They invited the family to dinner. The family accepted the invitation and they came to dinner not once but several times. The sisters and the family still have an ongoing relationship. In this way, a powerful message of the love of Jesus was sent by that grieving religious community to the community at large.

Many years ago, I attended a training institute on the RCIA. One of the presenting members of the team was a Washington, DC, pastor, Fr. Ray Kemp. He was pastor of St. Augustine's parish, one of the first parishes in the United States to offer the RCIA at that time. He and many others over the years, have preached that the "church" is not just in the pews but "out there" in the world, on the streets. Fr. Kemp boasted about the activities of this inner-city parish, predominantly African American. He said that every night of the week, the parish parking lot was full. He said every available room was used for activities such as RCIA, AA, OA, and NA. This parish was doing area outreach and meeting the needs of the community. I'm fairly certain not all the people in those parish rooms were Catholic or active Catholics.

Fr. Henri Nouwen wrote that hospitality offers us the opportunity to deepen and broaden our insight into our relationship to our fellow human beings; this is the core of discipleship. If we are to be disciples and minister to each other, we must be in relationship not only with those we come across each day, but also with our God (Knipper, p. 193).

The parish to which I belong has wonderful programs of

outreach to the community. One of the parish's full-time staff members is a minister of outreach. (And yes, outreach is the responsibility of all of us, but it helps to have some folks coordinate the ministry.)

A local faith-based community provides food and services to the poor in our county. They send a van to our church parking lot once a month, on a Sunday, and stay there all day. Parishioners, before and after Mass, drop off non-perishable food.

One week in January, we host a hypothermia clinic for service to the homeless. We feed them dinner, provide musical entertainment, bring in service dogs, and offer foot washing and haircuts. We provide gift cards to local restaurants and a "store" where they can get warm clothing and shoes. We serve breakfast, pack lunches, and, for most, drive them to their jobs or a daytime shelter. In the evening, we pick them up and return them to the parish where they spend the night. No parish activities are held that week as our eighty-plus guests fill up the entire building. Two other Catholic churches, some Protestant churches, and a Jewish synagogue also offer hypothermia weeks. The faith communities work in cooperation with Fairfax County, VA, which provides the vans and counselors. Thanks to this program, there have been hardly any more deaths from hypothermia. I am overwhelmed at the generosity of the hundreds of volunteers who make this program a reality. And what an incredible gospel message for the community at large.

Some of our younger Catholics (Generations X, Y, Z) criticize the Catholic Church for being all talk and no action. But when they see us living the social justice teachings of the church, they are more likely to be impressed as well as possibly think about returning.

Hospitality and Welcome to Couples Seeking the Sacrament of Marriage

Some critics say that the teachings of the church are no longer relevant to people's lives. I think if the church is going to be relevant, it needs to be there to help, support, grieve, and celebrate. A parish, as much as possible, needs to be present for all the significant events, both positive and negative.

For example, think of a young couple who has decided to marry in the church. They approach the parish and ask for an appointment to start their marriage preparation. Perhaps this couple has not been active in the church for a while. Perhaps one of them is not Catholic. Perhaps they have been living together, thinking that, since they were engaged, it was okay. The couple wants the wedding to be a wonderful celebration and their marriage to be successful. Not only are they watching to see what we do, both of their families, nuclear and extended, will be observing and passing judgment.

What are some of the tools, skills, and programs a parish needs to make this a loving, faith-filled time? First and foremost, the initial encounter of this couple with parish staff needs to be warm, inviting, and non-judgmental. There will be plenty of time (in most dioceses six months) to present the church's teachings on sexuality, marriage, and family life.

Ultimately, the moral decisions the couple makes are theirs to make. Our job is to help them form a Catholic conscience. They have come to us, and we would like them to stay. There are excellent marriage programs available that are affordable and user-friendly. These programs include topics that are essential to marriage—morality, sexuality, the sacrament of marriage, communication, finances, relationships with in-laws and extended family, aging parents, and parenting. A good program will recommend that both clergy and lay married people present and facilitate the sessions. I have worked in parishes where the actual wedding preparation is offered by someone not doing the marriage preparation. It could be someone from the liturgy and/or music staff who walks the couple through the selection of music, readings, etc. The parish I am in now has wedding coordinators who are on site for the rehearsal and the celebration of the sacrament. These people make sure all runs smoothly on the big day.

As I have mentioned before, I am totally convinced that if the parish is informed and conscientious about the preparation for and celebrations of all (or at least six) of the sacraments, people's lives and hearts will be touched and opened by the Holy Spirit. Often people who have left the church and have or witness a good sacramental experience will return. I have seen it happen so many times.

A Bouncing Baby Baptism

The next time the church is likely to hear from this couple is when they are expecting their first child. This contact is very important, but I also think there should be contact before then. Often, young couples live a great distance from their families of origin; maybe they are new in town and do not have the support system they might have if they were closer to home. It is important for them to have a place in the community. Some parishes have sponsor couples for newly married couples moving in. Parishes can reach out to them with wedding anniversary cards and young adult faith formation opportunities—online or at a local Starbucks or Panera. Some parishes offer small faith communities for young married couples.

I was a young wife and mother, married to a U.S. naval officer. We moved every eighteen months, and one of the first contacts I always made was with the local parish, which was usually very helpful as we settled in.

The young couple expecting their first child comes to the church and is told they need to register for infant baptism preparation sessions. This news may come a surprise to some of them. I have usually said to couples that just as they had formation for their marriage, it is also important to prepare themselves for the baptism of their child. They will be introducing their child to a lifelong journey of faith, and as church we wish to help them and accompany them on their journey. It is important for these young families to have the support they need.

Once again, it is important for parish staffs to be welcoming, not martinets. The couple and extended family will be affected by this process. There are many excellent programs and resources available. Keep the process short, simple, focused, and user-friendly. I would recommend no more than two sessions. Whether the couple is expecting or living with an infant, they are busy, stressed, and sleep-deprived. Invite the godparents, if local, to attend the sessions as well. I also think it is helpful to have a team of lay presenters facilitating the sessions. Members of this team (trained by professional catechetical staff) should range in age from young to middle age to older folks. The couples can identify with young parents who have just gone through the process but can also benefit from the wisdom and experience of grandparents who have raised their children and may be helping with their own grandchildren. All these folks can be very effective at witnessing to the value of Catholic life in their own family lives.

If your parish is blessed enough to have a parish nurse on staff, let your couples know this and let them know that the services provided are free. Parish nurses, in addition to providing immediate help and information, can be a great information resource for services available in the community.

Be sure your team is well informed about the laws (*Code of Canon Law*, 872–874) regarding the eligibility of godparents. Some parishes require of their godparents proof of baptism and confirmation and an assurance that the godparents have good Christian values and are actively practicing their faith. I have no problem with the requirements, but it is good to be aware that volatile issues may arise.

For example, a couple wants to invite "Aunt Tillie and Uncle Joe" to be the godparents. They go to Mass and volunteer in their parish, but it turns out Aunt Tillie was married before, and she and Joe were married in the Baptist church. Aunt Tillie was too nervous to get an annulment of her first marriage, and she never told anyone in the family that she was married before. Unfortunately, because of canon law on marriage, Aunt Tillie and Uncle Joe cannot serve as godparents. Aunt Tillie would have to get her first marriage annulled and her present marriage validated in the Catholic church. The expecting couple would need to invite others to be godparents, but they can still invite Aunt Tillie and Uncle Joe to attend the baptism. They can also, if Tillie and Joe are interested, give them a parish contact with whom they can talk about an annulment. This should be a gentle, loving, encouraging approach—no judgment.

Some cultures, such as Latino or Filipino, have many godparents at baptism. Invite them all, but select two who will act as the official godparents at the ceremony; list them all on the baptismal certificate, but designate the two official ones.

The parish staff should also be sensitive to the parent's wishes in planning the ceremony. For example, don't push baptism by immersion if the couple is more comfortable with pouring water, or vice versa. If the family prefers baptism in the chapel after Mass as opposed to during Mass, fine. We may understand the liturgical and theological significance of having the entire worshiping assembly witnessing the baptism and vowing to support the parents and godparents in their care of this child, but such a setting may be very intimidating to a family or a "not friendly" option for non-Catholic or non-practicing Catholic family members and friends. And remember, this sensitive approach may win some of them back.

Some parishes do not maintain contact with these families once the baby is baptized. I think the time between infancy and preschool (when some religious education programs start) can be a missed opportunity. Some parishes send families cards on the anniversary of their child's baptism. They note developmental accomplishments—"Congratulations, your child must be walking now…talking, etc." My parish offers a Mom's Group for mothers with young children. They meet in the parish nursery. The kids play, and the moms discuss spirituality, Scripture, and parenting; they exchange phone numbers of babysitters and just generally support each other. Your parish may offer family or intergenerational catechesis—something for everyone. Babysitters are provided for really little ones, and the rest of the family—kids, parents, grandparents—attends catechetical sessions, sometimes together as families, sometimes in age-appropriate groups, or sometimes in a combination of both. (I also discovered that the secret to a successful RCIA adapted for children was family catechesis. Parents were getting the catechesis and community support they needed and were encouraged to work with their children at home.)

If all of this is done well, some folks return to an active practice of the faith. This is a program that helps families to feel that the church is relevant to their lives, that we are dealing with issues with which they deal. Yes, some of these services are provided in the community at large but they are not faith-based communities, and that is what many families seek.

When I was hired at a parish in Northern Virginia in the mid-eighties, the pastor asked me to start the RCIA. I did happily and my plan was to start the process for adults and then expand it to include children. Two years after I was hired, I approached the pastor and asked permission to implement the rite for children.

I started the process, and eventually the "word on the street" was if you haven't baptized your child and/or haven't brought your children in for first penance, first Eucharist, or confirmation, bring them to St. B's. The staff doesn't scold you or make you feel guilty; they just warmly welcome you and do what they can to help. The process grew, and we had many children. In two more years, we started the process Re-Membering Church (a model based on the RCIA, but the focus is on reconciliation and a return to the church, not baptism and entrance into the church). So now we had a process for returning parents and anyone else who wanted to return.

Many years ago, when I worked for the Archdiocese of Baltimore, I worshiped at a parish in Columbia, Maryland. This parish was using the Re-Membering Church process. I had also, as I just mentioned, used this process when I worked at a parish in Springfield, Virginia. The RCIA is a restoration, with adaptation of course, of the catechumenate of the early church. Re-Membering Church, is a restoration, again with adaptation, of the order of penitents from the early church. The focus of the catechumenate is initiation, and the focus of Re-Membering Church is reconciliation.

In Re-Membering Church, there is an introductory and formation process; then the immediate preparation is the liturgical season of Lent. Lent, of course, started as preparation for baptism, and later it also included the already baptized as they prepared for a renewal of their baptismal commitment. At Mass on Ash Wednesday, penitents wishing to return to the church received ashes, embraced the cross, and asked for the community's love and support. Their six weeks, not unlike that of the Elect, were spent in prayer, fasting, and faith sharing. On Holy Thursday, at the celebration of the Last Supper, the penitents processed in and were invited to reverence the altar. They were embraced by the clergy and the parish staff and, at this point, the members of the assembly were invited to embrace them as well. It was a very powerful ritual. They then participated in the rest of the liturgy, including, at last, receiving the Eucharist.

Forgiveness and Reconciliation
As I have mentioned earlier, preparation for and celebration of the sacraments are key teachable and transformative moments. Some adults are not well catechized about the sacrament of penance or have had a negative experience of it. Often parents will enroll their children in the process preparing them to receive first penance, but they themselves want nothing to do

with the sacrament. Most parishes require parent participation for their children's reception of the sacraments. I'm not a big fan of mandatory attendance, but if they do come, it gives us an opportunity to give them a picture, and an experience, of a merciful God who loves them unconditionally and will forgive all their sins.

Pope Francis has much to say on this topic of unconditional love and forgiveness. A few days before his election as pope, then Cardinal Bergoglio preached on John's gospel story of the adulteress. During the homily, he told a story of a conversation he had had with a man who said he "had done terrible things." The man thought himself as "irredeemable." The pope's reply to him was this: "Go to Jesus. He likes to hear about these things. He forgets; he has a special knack for forgetting. He forgets, he kisses you, embraces you, and he says, 'Neither do I condemn you. Go, and from now on do not sin anymore.' That is the only advice he gives. If things haven't changed in a month…we go back to the Lord. The Lord never tires of forgiving: never!" "This is the face of the church that doesn't reproach [persons] for their fragility and their wounds but that treats them with the medicine of mercy" (Tornielli, p. xi).

A year later, the pope, at a Mass at St. Martha's House, returned to the same gospel and said, "God forgives not with a decree but with a caress…Jesus too goes beyond the law and forgives by caressing the wounds of our sins" (Tornielli, pp. xii and xiii).

"Like the father of the prodigal son waiting with open arms, all we need to do, like the prodigal son, is take a step toward him…even the desire to take a step is enough" (Tornielli, p. xix).

When I'm talking with folks who are anxious about receiving the sacrament of reconciliation, I often ask them to picture Christ, down the road, waiting with open arms to embrace them. They are the son or daughter running (or walking hesitantly) toward him for his embrace of love and forgiveness.

By now, most have heard of Pope Francis' wonderful image of the church as a "field hospital: a mobile structure that offers first aid and immediate care, so that its soldiers do not die. It's a place for urgent care.... [It is] a Church that goes forth toward those who are wounded, who are in need of an attentive ear, understanding, forgiveness, and love" (Tornielli, p. 53). I also like the pope's use of the phrase "apostolate of the ear."

These are words that need to be shared with our returnees. The thoughts are so comforting for all of us.

Connecting with the Disconnected as You Minister to Their Growing Children

Some parents want this forgiveness not just for themselves but also for their children. In the years I directed these programs, it was not uncommon at the celebration of the sacrament for parents to receive as well. We invited them to return and receive the sacrament, even after an absence of many years. It was wonderful to be a part of the process that really enabled them to experience the unconditional, merciful love of God. Many, many times, in parishes where I worked, confessors at the family penance services would tell me that some of their adult penitents had been away from the sacrament for ten, twenty, even thirty years. Some catechists and parishioners felt that the service should be only for the children. I disagreed because I felt it was a wonderful opportunity for their parents to receive—and in some cases return to regular reception of—the sacrament. We did a small family group dismissal rite, so no one had to wait a long time for the end of the service. Priests and staff were also conscientious about needed follow-up, and we still had the first Eucharist preparation program for them to experience as well.

When I worked for the Archdiocese of Baltimore, I was accepted into the National Catholic Education Association National Scholars Program. This was a two-year study and research program. We spent two weeks for two summers studying at The Catholic University of America in Washington, DC, and Loyola University in New Orleans with some of the finest Catholic minds in this country.

In the intervening time, we were to research a selected topic and end with a paper. The *General Directory for Catechesis* had just been published, and many of us were very happy that this document stated that the baptismal catechumenate should be the model for all catechesis. We knew the catechumenate process worked but were struggling with the concept of how, practically speaking, it would work in other forms of catechesis. Not knowing any better, I chose that question for my research topic.

The topic, of course, was huge, so I narrowed it down to parish preparation programs for first penance and first Eucharist. I selected three parishes that I knew had a good understanding and practice of both sound catechesis and the baptismal catechumenate. I asked the directors of religious education at these parishes to restructure their sacramental preparation programs to reflect the principles of the RCIA. At the end of the year's process, I developed a questionnaire for them to give to the parents so they could evaluate the process. One of the questions asked was, if they had been away from the church, did they return or were they thinking about returning? These are some of the responses from parents.

> My faith has deepened as I learned from my son. We do more family ritual now. I have a better understanding of the values of the church. I have renewed my own beliefs in the church. I was away from the church for twenty years, and the birth of my son, who is now preparing for first Eucharist, brought me back. The retreat helped me to see the sacrament through my son's eyes. I will always cherish the memories of the time I spent with my family and our church family.
>
> Faith and being a Catholic have been struggles for me. I really got more than I expected from the program. The church has changed since the 1960s…it's changing for the better.

One parent who returned to the church because of his involvement with his child's sacramental preparation gave a powerful witness talk at one of the parent meetings. The DRE now plans to invite one of these parents to do this every year.

> I grew closer to my child and went to confession myself for the first time in twenty years. It was an experience of the examination of conscience for parents as well as the children. The experience brought my family closer together and individual relationships within the family were strengthened. Your program created opportunities for families to discuss issues of right and wrong. It provided an opportunity for me to reflect on my own spirituality. It was a renewal of the experience of God's forgiveness. God really does forgive sins.

In our sacramental preparation programs, we were very conscious of being welcoming and gracious to non-Catholic parents and non-practicing Catholic parents. They were invited to all events; and at the first Eucharist Mass, families sat together with their first communicant, and all family members and guests were invited to accompany the child as he or she received the Eucharist. Non-receiving adults simply indicated to the priest or Eucharistic minister that they were not receiving by crossing their arms across their chest. Instead, they received a blessing. (This practice is more common in parishes now as we become more sensitive to our families' needs.) This generosity of spirit is a marked change from some past practices and goes a long way toward easing folks back to the church.

Another practice that seems to be evolving in the Catholic Church is giving the adolescent candidate for confirmation the option to decide whether or not he/she wants to be confirmed. Some parents, clergy, and catechists were upset with this practice, but no lasting good is accomplished by holding young people hostage to the sacrament. The Holy Spirit and the church are not going anywhere—they will always be there for these youngsters. It is better to introduce them to a loving relationship with the triune God and his church and allow them the right and privilege to respond to God's call to love and commit to the faith when they are ready. Most kids decide to proceed with the sacrament (even though my three daughters thought I was kidding when I gave them the option). The few who opted out knew they were not ready, but in a year or two they requested the sacrament. God, as we know, is very persistent in his call. Read Psalm 139 or Francis Thompson's poem "The Hound of Heaven" or even Margaret Wise Brown's

The Runaway Bunny. At some point, often sooner rather than later, these young people will hunger for and receive the Spirit of Jesus in their lives. Too many of our folks, as youngsters or young adults, leave the church because they were "strong armed" or felt their dignity and freedom were not respected. Jesus wants us to love him and live his love willingly and freely. It is the only valid response.

The Sick and Bereaved

Now we come to visits to the homebound, the sacrament of the sick, viaticum, ministry to the dying, funerals, and burials. I started out this book with a story of the angry daughter of a woman who died without the rites of the church and a priest to administer them. Being sick, alone, and in pain—or being the loved ones of that person—is a painful, needy, and vulnerable experience. This is definitely a time when the loving, healing presence of Christ is needed.

We are the ones who bring Christ to the sick, the dying, and the grieving, not just in the Eucharist or in the word but in ourselves. I had a priest friend, now in heaven with Jesus, who was a chaplain at a local hospital. Often when the calls came from the hospital, his sleep was interrupted and he had to go out in the middle of the night. When he experienced the normal, human reaction of "I just want to stay in my warm bed," he would look at a statue he kept on his night table. It was a statue of Jesus, the Good Shepherd, and the lost sheep. "Jesus would go out and take care of his sheep," Fr. Paul would say to himself, "and so must I." Fr. Paul was a wise, kind, and tender man.

I'm sure many Catholic friends and families of the sick and dying to whom Fr. Paul ministered returned to the church because of his merciful and loving presence. Fr. Paul is a hard act to follow but that is who we are called to be. I have had the privilege of bringing the Eucharist to the sick, both in their homes and in the hospital. I have had the privilege of helping family members plan the funeral of a loved one, helping them pick the Scriptures and music. I have listened to the stories of the quirks, loving nature, funny stories, and the faith of the deceased. This information was used to help personalize the rites for them and the worshiping community. It was a healing experience for them and for me.

Just recently, a mother of one of our neophytes, a young college student, suffered a brain hemorrhage and died within a few days. She was only sixty years old. The RCIA team and several members of the parish offered many prayers, and all of us attended the funeral Mass. I sang in the choir at the Mass. The liturgy was really beautiful. The husband of this woman had left the church a few years ago. He had been attending a parish in another city. When they moved to our town, he could not find a parish that he liked, so he stopped attending Mass. The Sunday after her burial, the husband, his two sons, and his extended family attended the Mass the RCIA folks usually attend, and after Mass they all joined us for coffee and donuts. The husband said to us that he wished to return to the church, in this parish, and he wanted to get involved in ministry. He did not say why, but I can only assume he was pleased with the experience his son had had in the RCIA and his own experience of the parish community during his wife's illness, death, and burial.

I refer to the parish front desk (or reception desk) as "front line" ministry. How the walk-in visitor is received is critical. The person coming may not always be warm and friendly. They may have a "beef" or an issue. When faced with rudeness, it is not always easy for the staff person at the desk to be warm and kind. Often our first instinct is to "react" to the attitude or mood of the person coming in. The staff person's job is to be Christlike. I realized maintaining that attitude requires a lot of prayer and grace. But if we want that person to stay or return, that is the attitude required. I have tremendous admiration for the personnel "on the front lines."

As a religious educator, I am a big advocate of lifelong faith formation. For years, the normative way for parishes to provide this catechesis was on site, in classrooms—some of them "adult friendly"—or in people's homes. I still think the best way for adults to learn and share faith is through personal interaction, but in today's culture and fast-paced society that mode is not only not convenient but also not realistic. I have watched one of my daughters rearrange her whole day and work schedule (including enlisting me as a babysitter) so that she could attend a 6:30 PM (really? 6:30?) parent meeting for first sacraments. She could just as easily have received the information in an electronic document, watched a video, or even chatted with other parents and the DRE in a chat room or a GoToMeeting format—much easier and more convenient.

Online catechesis can be provided on a parish or diocesan website or even YouTube or Vimeo sites if they are appropriate. If someone is thinking of returning to the church and is not yet ready to make a public appearance, he or she can go online. There are, of course, some websites that are bizarre or not always authentically Catholic. Controlling access to these sites is impossible, but the DRE can list websites that are highly recommended to guide our seekers. The job description of the

DRE has to change to include the ability to research, monitor, and recommend catechetically sound websites. This kind of expertise requires hours of research as one sifts through and sorts sites, but the time spent is well worth the effort.

Also, the parish website can list information on supportive activities for seniors, youth, families, divorced and separated folks, and those who grieve. Also, when folks call or email inquiring about some of these activities, or maybe volunteer to help, be sure that someone on the staff responds to them quickly. Many times, I have heard the statement, "I called and no one got back to me."

Welcome the LGBTQI Community

In the first chapter, I referred to the church's embrace of LGBTQI individuals. I know of a bishop, Bishop Burbidge, now in the Diocese of Arlington, formerly bishop of the Diocese of Raleigh, NC, who, as most bishops do, makes parish visits. In one parish in the Diocese of Raleigh, when he visited the parish, he made a point of visiting the support group for LGBTQI Catholics. I'm sure he didn't announce or promote a change in the church's teachings, but his visible support certainly made a strong statement about his love and support for their dignity as persons loved by God.

Chapter Five

SHARING OUR PASTORAL PRACTICES WITH YOU

When I was in the NCEA Scholars Program, one of our presenters was Matthew Hayes. I remember one of his quotes, and I think it is relevant for this chapter. He defined critical reflection as the willingness to look at why things (programs) succeed or not; the willingness to shift paradigms; the willingness to examine why we do the same things over and over and expect different results (NCEA Scholars Program, CUA, 1999). A "non-starter" statement in leadership and management is, "But we have always done it this way!" That kind of thinking gets us nowhere. I challenge you as parish staffs to think "outside the box" or as Matt would say, "shift paradigms."

I have discovered that the approach does not have to be complicated or expensive. There are many programs available for the Welcome Home process and they are listed in the appendix, but let me describe the simple approach we use.

Recently I met with the coordinator, a volunteer lay man, of the Welcome Home process in our parish. He and the pastor, the director of faith formation, and a lay woman who returned to the church a few years ago are members of the team. The process is offered three or four times a year. Anywhere from six to ten adults return each year, ranging in age from their twenties to their seventies. Most, however, are in their twenties and thirties. I asked the reasons people left. The coordinator said:

- some just drifted away, often during college years
- parents didn't attend church
- illness—theirs or that of a parent
- the death of a loved one
- divorce

As I mentioned before, northern Virginia is a bedroom community for Washington, DC. The population in general is highly intelligent, upper middle class, well educated, culturally diverse, and very transient. The younger folks do not always have local family support.

The folks in our program have been away from the church for an average of seven to twelve years. The group meets for four to six weeks. The coordinator for this process also coordinates the inquiry process for the RCIA. The process he uses is somewhat similar—the obvious difference being the focus on returning, not entering, on reconciliation, not initiation. The coordination is very low-key and nurturing; the coordinator is very skilled at putting people at ease and helping them to feel safe. They meet in a parish room that is very adult friendly—small, cozy, homey. He starts with basic introductions and then asks questions such as "What are you looking for? "What do you need?" He eventually extends an invitation to tell their story. He does not use a published book or series. He does focus on forgiveness, spirituality, and their relationship with God. The team will also, at some point, do informal catechesis on the liturgy, do a tour of the church and sacristy, and offer catechesis on the sacraments, especially reconciliation. He points out that receiving the sacrament of reconciliation will be one of the last things they do, if they are ready. It is not advisable to encourage reception of this sacrament until they have had some time in the program.

One of the topics discussed near the end of the process is a discussion of ministries. What ministries are available in the parish and the community and what might be a good fit for them. This is not so much a recruitment pitch as a way to help them feel part of the parish. The parish is huge (12,000 people) and to get involved is a way of being a part of the many little churches within the big church. It is also a way to become part of a smaller faith community that will continue to support them. One of the team members, who was away from the church for many years and then returned in this parish, shares her story of why she left, why and how she returned, and who helped her (her story is in the first chapter of this book). In one session, the team members share their favorite Scripture stories.

When they are ready, those attending the program are gently encouraged to attend Mass—an invitation not an obligation. The following week, the team asks: What was the one thing they took away from the liturgy—a word, a phrase, a song? During the sessions, the team uses large-group sharing and one-on-one conversations.

The coordinator gave me this quote, which he often uses: "No one cares how much you know until you know how much we care." It is a great quote and so reassuring.

At the last session, they talk about arranging to receive the sacrament of penance, if they are ready and want to receive it. The team recommends that they make an appointment with one of the priests instead of just getting in the "Saturday line." The team follows up with a phone call, a meeting, if desired, and registration in the parish.

I asked what the process still needed. The leader said better marketing and publicity, especially in terms of a parish-wide effort toward evangelization. Evangelization, like initiation, is the business of all the baptized. He also mentioned the need for more staff and volunteer support. In a large parish such as this one, this process needs more than a handful of people to help.

Lastly, but not in importance, is the welcome desk, which can be either a place of welcome and hospitality or the first line of resistance. The same thinking applies to the inquiring phone call or email. And, if for some reason, the inquiry needs to be referred to a staff or team member, be sure they get back to the inquirer as soon as possible. You do not want to send the message that we don't care about you.

Chapter Six

A Look at Your Pastoral Practices

This chapter is devoted to helping the parish staff examine their procedures, from how they answer the phone to sacramental policies. As you read through this chapter, you may want to reflect on how well you are doing. None of us is perfect—there is always room for growth and improvement. See if you can identify your strengths as well as your challenges. This chapter (and book) could serve as the basis for a leadership retreat for your staff, pastoral council, and finance council. As part of this retreat, small groups could gather to process their areas of expertise and responsibility. I have always found gatherings such as these very helpful for my ministries. The affirmation felt good, and the challenges helped me to focus my energy, time, and prayer.

Staff, Hospitality, Maintenance
For all staff members and volunteers, hospitality and availability are key. As I have mentioned before, be sure you are friendly and helpful in answering the phone and emails, as well as when dealing with walk-ins and visitors.

Be sure your parish registration forms are user-friendly and that your Mass and confession schedules are well publicized. Some parishes publish their schedules in the local newspaper. A staff/parish directory and welcome packets are useful, not just for newcomers but for all parishioners. If you have a tech-savvy web master, ask them to design a parish website that is attractive, informative, and user-friendly. Use similar guidelines for your parish bulletin—informative, attractive, not cluttered. Go online and look at other parish websites and bulletins—research and comparisons can be helpful.

Relatively simple things like good signage leading to your campus, signage on buildings, names on the rooms, directional arrows, adequate lighting inside and out, and adequate parking can be extremely helpful and welcoming. Put a map of your campus on the website. The last parish where I worked was bordered by two cul-de-sacs and sat on the edge of dense wooded area. It was a beautiful setting but very hard to find; not even GPS knew where it was. Landscape and snow removal services are expensive but essential. Are all your buildings accessible for persons with physical disabilities?

Lastly, all parish staff and parishioners need to make a conscious effort to be a warm and welcoming community and committed to building community. (When I moved to the DC area from Virginia Beach, it was eight months before anyone even spoke to me in my new parish.) If you do not have a parish mission statement, you might want to consider writing one. Part of the mission statement of my parish is "All are welcome!" That statement is a lived reality—some people travel long distances to worship with us. People in our RCIA and Welcome Home processes often say, "You are such a welcoming community—I feel at home here!"

Faith Formation
For the faith formation director, director of religious education, and coordinator of RCIA, and other such ministries, the same advice applies to paperwork. Put all your registration forms online—religious education registration, vacation Bible school, sacramental preparation, adult faith formation, Welcome Home. Make the forms user-friendly and have some hard copies printed out for walk-ins, new parishioners, or folks who do not have electronic devices.

The catechetical documents of our church state that the primary, most important form of catechesis is that of adults. It is important to offer them a variety of venues and formats. If you don't already offer it, you might want to consider offering family/intergenerational catechesis. It is a refreshing change from just the classroom model; it brings neighborhoods and small faith communities together and may very well involve non-Catholics and inactive Catholics. Also, effective ways to catechize the adults are with retreats and seasonal parish missions (e.g., in Lent). Invite everybody! And as I mentioned earlier, do not forget our children, youth, and adults with intellectual disabilities—they want to meet Jesus and be a part of the faith community too.

Liturgy and Music

Every parish needs to have a director of liturgy and a director of music. Ideally these positions should be two separate people who work closely together. (Not every parish has the financial freedom to offer two separate positions). There should be a liturgy committee, comprised of the pastor, clergy, both directors, and parishioners. I've discovered it is a good idea to provide liturgical formation to the volunteers.

The primary task of this committee is to plan Sunday liturgies, especially by liturgical season. Someone needs to be in charge of the environment. It is nice to have greeters at the door. Acknowledge and welcome newcomers and visitors right before Mass begins. Staff the welcome desk so that questions/concerns can be addressed before and after Mass. These latter items may seem obvious, but they go a long way toward building community and providing a welcoming environment.

The liturgy director coordinates the ministries of lectors, servers, and extraordinary ministers of the Eucharist. The music director, usually, coordinates the cantors, choirs, and musicians. A vital role for the liturgy director is to coordinate the ministry of bringing the Eucharist to the sick and homebound and those in hospitals, nursing homes, and rehabilitation centers. The clergy usually does this visitation, especially if it involves the sacrament of the sick, but in the parish the size of mine (3,500 households) the clergy can use a little help! Also under the purview of the liturgy director could be wedding and funeral coordinators. Since so many different spiritualities/devotions exist in our Catholic tradition, it is nice to offer sessions on praying the Rosary, adoration, contemplative prayer, etc.

Pastoral and efficient execution of these ministries will undoubtedly nurture the faith of active members and help people to return to an active practice of their faith.

Outreach
A most important parish ministry is outreach to the community—both local and global. This is a parish-wide mission, but it helps to have someone on staff to coordinate it because it is so vast and has so many different components. In a small parish, the coordinator may be clergy, pastoral associate, or DRE. In a larger parish, with more financial resources, such as mine, it can be a full-time staff person. This person may coordinate programs such as Welcome Home, evangelization, outreach to other faith communities, and programs for the separated and divorced and bereaved. A parish can have family nights with an ice cream social and family friendly movies. A parish can offer multicultural activities, such as an Our Lady of Guadalupe festival.

For several years now, our parish has offered the JustFaith course on the Catholic social teachings of the church. Its graduates and other parishioners sponsor and help run activities such as a fair trade fair. Some become involved in services to refugees and immigrants. Some parishioners have established a program called "Care for Our Common Home," which does direct service to the local community as well as consciousness raising and education on our responsibility to take care of and improve our climate and environment.

Finance

The finance council does more than count money. The council is the financial steward of the parish. If the parish is a life-giving community, the money will come in, even in middle- to lower-income communities. Offer your communities the option of electronic contributions; such a process makes it much easier to project income and plan a realistic budget. It is good if you can budget monies for conferences for your staff and volunteer leaders. And every parish, regardless of size, has an obligation to be stewards themselves and set aside money for the poor. Some larger parishes are able to adopt a mission parish in this country, or in Latin America, South America, and overseas. Such global outreach is an inspiring witness.

I know this a lot of material, and I am sure that there are items I have forgotten. In case you are wondering why I have included some of these items, it is because, as a parish, you are judged on all of the above. Someone is going to be impacted by at least one or two, if not more, of these areas. I did most of my career in religious education in the parish and on the diocesan level, but I did do one stint as a lay pastor. I used to sit at Mass in the church where I was pastor and count all the lightbulbs that had burnt out in the ceiling and needed to be replaced! Not meaningful worship, I admit, but significant nevertheless. You have to be able to see in church. Running a parish is multifaceted to say the least.

All these items take time, money, staff, and lots of volunteers. I have given you a list for the ideal parish—something we all work toward. I will say that having a strategic plan in place helps. Set goals five, ten, even twenty years out and devise a plan to get there. And pray! You want a well-functioning and welcoming parish not just for your parishioners but also for those coming back or even just thinking about coming back. You want to hear the comment, "I heard you all are such a warm and welcoming parish so I decided to come and check you out. And, guess what, you really are!"

The Welcome Home Process
Now it is time to form your team for your Welcome Home process. Team members are similar to RCIA sponsors. They do not have to be "mini-theologians"; there are staff people who can supply that kind of knowledge. They do, however, have to be practicing Catholics who are excited about their faith and eager to share it. They need to be good listeners and willing to share their own faith; they also need to recognize the Holy Spirit working in their lives and the lives of others.

Once you have formed your team, it is time to train them. On pages 74 and 75 is a sample agenda of what a couple of team training sessions might look like. Pages 76-78 display a sample agenda for a Welcome Home session.

SESSION 1

1. Welcome and thank you for coming *(5 minutes)*

2. Opening prayer and then a Scripture passage on mercy and forgiveness (I have listed some suggested passages in the appendix). Perhaps some sharing or *lectio divina* as part of or even the whole process. *(20 minutes)*

3. Open forum / discussion on some of the following: *(20–25 minutes)*

   - Appropriate attitudes to have toward returning Catholics
   - Some reasons why Catholics leave
   - Why they return—what are they looking for?
   - Do they know anyone who has left? Returned?
   - What are their hopes for the future?
   - What do they think the church could do to break down some of the barriers between Catholics who have left and the church?

4. Facilitator summarizes discussion *(5 minutes)*

5. Closing prayer *(5 minutes)*

TOTAL: *55-60 minutes*

A Look at Your Pastoral Practices 75

SESSION 2

1. Welcome *(5 minutes)*

2. Opening prayer, Scripture, sharing *(15 minutes)*

3. Thoughts/questions from first session *(5–10 minutes)*

4. Facilitator presentation: *(20 minutes)*

   - Importance of being good listeners (listening from the heart)
   - Sharing their faith
   - Not imposing their style of spirituality on others; the importance of the returnees finding their own path
   - Not blaming, not judging, not attempting to solve their problems
   - Emphasizing God's love and mercy and allowing the Holy Spirit to work in their lives
   - Review with them what a sample session might look like

5. Agenda of sample session to follow *(20 minutes)*

6. Questions / concerns *(5 minutes)*

7. Closing prayer *(5 minutes)*

TOTAL: *75-80 minutes*

Sample Agenda for Welcome Home Session

Pre-instructions for the parish staff and coordinator: When they receive inquiries, give contact information: address and phone number of the church, directions to the church and the building and room in which they meet. Have someone at the door to greet them and take them to the meeting room. Be sure that the room is adult friendly with subdued lighting. Provide name tags and markers. Have some simple refreshments available, such as coffee, tea, water, soft drinks, cookies, snacks, fruit, and put out paper and pens or pencils. Set up a prayer table with a cloth, candle, the Bible in the center, and perhaps a seasonal decoration or flowers. Provide comfortable seating.

AGENDA

1. Welcome, introductions, an ice breaker, opening remarks *(10 minutes)*

2. Explain the plan of the meeting—helps to calm people who may be anxious about what to expect *(5 minutes)*

3. Assure them that anything shared in the meeting is confidential

4. Invite people to tell their story about why they left and what happened to get them thinking about returning, if they feel comfortable doing

so. It might help to ask a team member who has left and returned to share their story first. Be non-reactive to their stories except for attentive, loving listening. *(20 minutes)*

5. Short break *(5 minutes)*

6. Brief presentation on a topic—maybe the Scripture of the day or the liturgical season; a brief introduction to the Mass; a homily by Pope Francis on forgiveness and mercy *(10 minutes)*

7. Prepare one or two discussion questions for the group to share on the topic presented *(10 minutes)*

8. Ask what topics they might want to hear about in future sessions *(10 minutes)*

9. Tell them of topics you have in mind, such as the Mass, the liturgical year, tour of the church, sacristy, Mary, sacramentals, devotions, changes in the church. Also, topics on the church's position on current events, such as immigration, refugees, war, social justice, and annulments *(5 minutes)*

(Note: A presentation on the annulment process would be very helpful to some folks. If one of your clergy or lay staff is an advocate for petitioners, have him or her speak or get a member of the diocesan tribunal to give a presentation.)

This may be a session you want to open to the entire parish as there is such a need to disseminate accurate information about this process).

10. Close with the Our Father (in future sessions you could ask the group for petitions)   *(5 minutes)*

TOTAL SESSION: *80 minutes*

In future sessions, you may want to do some one-on-one sharing on a topic—pair a returnee with a team member. At another session, have the returnees pair up with each other.

Provide the returning folks with journals, to take notes at the sessions and possibly write reflections at home to record their journey. This tool may appeal to some and not others.

If your pastor or another priest is not at all the meetings, be sure to invite him for the presentation on the sacrament of penance. This presentation seems to carry more credibility when given by a confessor.

If you wish to use a published program, I list resources at the end of the book. The process I have outlined above, however, seems to work very well. Also, you can use published resources as a guide and freely adapt what works best for your group and parish.

For doctrinal content, you should have at your disposal the *Catechism of the Catholic Church* and the *United States Catholic Catechism for Adults*, the latter easy for returnees to use. Another "user-friendly" resource for adults thinking of returning is

Believing in Jesus by Leonard Foley, OFM, from Franciscan Media. I am not suggesting we overload folks with doctrine, but it is important to offer them resources. The latter two resources are easy reading and easy to use if they want to look up a teaching or get ready answers to some of their questions.

Conclusion
I hope this book is helpful for those of you who do pastoral ministry to those returning to the church. Most of it is common sense and some of the ideas simply come from my years of experience. Two of the virtues St. Francis de Sales emphasized are patience and gentleness. Both are needed in ministry, especially when working with those returning to the church. One of the most difficult lessons for me to learn was that God works on his timetable, not mine. But the good news is that he does work; so let him lead, and you follow. God bless all of you who do his work!

APPENDIX

QUOTES AND SCRIPTURE PASSAGES THAT MAY BE HELPFUL

"Eye speaks to eye and heart speaks to heart, and no one understands what passes, save the sacred lovers who speak." — St. Francis De Sales, *Treatise on the Love of God, Book VI, 1*

The story of the tax collector—*Matthew 9:9–13*

The story of the prodigal son—*Luke 15:11–32*

The Samaritan woman at the well—*John 4:4–42*

The loaves and fishes—*Luke 9:10–17*

Jesus' forgiveness of Peter—*John 21:15–19*

The adulterous woman—*John 8:1–11*

SOME IMAGES OF GOD FROM SCRIPTURE

Were not our hearts burning within us?—*Luke 24:32*

Like a weaned child on its mother's lap, so is my soul within me.—*Psalm 131:2*

I have called you by name and you are mine.—*Isaiah 43:1*

The Lord called me from birth, from my mother's womb he gave me my name.—*Isaiah 49:1*

Can a mother forget her infant, be without tenderness for her

child? Yet even should she forget, I will never forget you.
—*Isaiah 49:15*

See, I have written your name on the palms of my hands.
—*Isaiah 49:16*

Hide me in the shadow of your wings.—*Psalm 17:8*

And he would have given you living water.—*John 4:10*

Do not be afraid any longer, for our Father is pleased to give you the kingdom.—*Luke 12:32*

For you my soul thirsts.—*Psalm 63:1 (verse 2 in some Bibles)*

Set me as a seal on your heart.—*Song of Songs 8:6*

SOME SUGGESTED DISCUSSION QUESTIONS

- Do we always feel open to God's love, responsive, worthy?
- Do we trust in God's personal love and care for us?
- Are we as gentle and forgiving of ourselves as God is of us?
- God gazes upon me (Psalm 139): how open am I to receiving this intimacy?
- Do I trust God, even in the tough times?

RESOURCES FOR WELCOMING HOME RETURNING CATHOLICS

- **Landings International: Welcome Returning Catholics**
  published by the Paulist Fathers. The website for the program (www.landingsinternational.org) has a description of the program and where to find one. It also has questions such as, *Do I have to go back to confession first before I go back to Mass? What if I am divorced...?* and the answers.

  The Paulists also have a newer program (2000), *Awakening Faith: Reconnecting with Your Catholic Faith*, a Small Group Process for Inactives.

- **Online Catholic educational sites**
  e.g, Catholic Distance Learning—www.cdu.edu; classes available online.

- **Diocesan newspapers**
  source of good information on the Catholic faith.

- **Sunday readings**:
  Living with Christ (www.livingwithchrist.us)
  The Word Among Us (www.wau.org)
  Give Us This Day (www.giveusthisday.org)

- **More Catholic resources on daily readings and news**
  www.catholic.org—Sunday readings, daily readings, documents of the Church

- **American bishops' website**
  www.usccb.org will email free daily readings

- **Catholics Come Home**
  (www.catholicscomehome.org) for former Catholics

- **Catholics Come Home: I'm not currently attending Mass**
  www.catholicscomehome.org/not-attending-Mass.

- **Find a Mass near you**
  www.masstimes.org

- **Busted Halo**
  an online magazine for spiritual seekers
  (www.bustedhalo.com)

- **Sacred Space Prayer website**
  daily prayer online (Irish Jesuits and Loyola Press) plus free apps

- **Center for Action and Contemplation**
  (www.cac.org) Fr. Richard Rohr, OFM, offers daily meditations online, events, conferences, adult faith formation

- **You Can Go Home Again: Resources for Returning Catholics**
  www.uscatholic.org/you-can-go-home-again-resources-returning-catholics.

BIBLIOGRAPHY

Augustine of Hippo. *The Confessions*, Book One, Chapter One. New York: Washington Square Press, 1951.

Brennan, Patrick. *The Evangelizing Parish*. San Antonio, TX: Tabor Publishing, 1987.

Brown, Margaret Wise. *The Runaway Bunny*. New York: Harper, 1942.

Canon Law Society of America. *Code of Canon Law*, Latin and English ed., second translation. Washington, DC: Libreria Editrice Vaticana Rome, 1983, 1989 (first translation of the new code).

Congregation for Divine Worship. *General Directory for Catechesis*, English ed., second edition. Washington, DC: USCCB Publishing, 2005.

De Sales, St. Francis. *Treatise on the Love of God*, Book VI, 1, translated by Rt. Rev. John K. Ryan. Stella Niagara, NY: DeSales Resource Center, 2010.

Foley, Leonard, OFM. *Believing in Jesus*, fifth revised edition. Cincinnati: St. Anthony Messenger Press, 2005.

Harmony, Sarah. *Re-Membering: The Ministry of Welcoming Alienated and Inactive Catholics*. Collegeville, MN: Liturgical Press, 1991.

International Committee on English in the Liturgy and the Bishops' Committee on the Liturgy, USCCB. *The Rite of Christian Initiation of Adults: The Roman Ritual*, English ed. Archdiocese of Chicago. Chicago: Liturgy Training Publications, 1988.

Knipper, Deacon Jim, ed. *Naked and You Clothed Me: Homilies and Reflections for Cycle C*, 16th Sunday in Ordinary Time, Manalpan, NJ: Clear Vision Publishing, 2012.

Kordes, Marie and Spayd, Loyes. *Apprenticeship in Christian Life: Explaining the Baptismal Catechumenate as Inspiration for All Catechesis*. Washington, DC: National Conference for Catechetical Leadership and The North American Forum on the Catechumenate, 2005.

Paulist National Catholic Evangelization Association (PNCEA). *Landings: Welcoming Returning Catholics*, designed by Fr. Jac Campbell, North American Paulist Center, 3031 Fourth St. NE, Washington, DC: 1991.

Rolheiser, Ronald. *The Holy Longing: The Search for a Christian Spirituality*. New York: The Crown Publishing Group, 2014.

Special Religious Development (SPRED), Archdiocese of Chicago (info@SPRED.org).

Thompson, Francis. "The Hound of Heaven," in *The Oxford Book of English Mystical Verse*, eds., Nicholson and Lee: 1917.

Tornielli, Andrea and Pope Francis. *The Name of God Is Mercy* (Homily), March 7, 2013. New York: Random House, 2016.

United States Conference of Catholic Bishops (USCCB), Pope John Paul II. *Catechesi Tradendae (On Catechesis in Our Time)*. Washington, DC: 1979.

USCCB. *Catechism of the Catholic Church*, second edition, English, ed. Washington, DC: 1997.

USCCB. *United States Catholic Catechism for Adults*. Washington, DC: 2007.

Wright, Wendy. *Heart Speaks to Heart: The Salesian Tradition*. Maryknoll, NY: Orbis Books, 2004.